be kind

30 DEVOTIONS FOR DEVELOPING
THE HEART GOD DESIRES

Published by LifeWay Press®

No part of this work may be reproduced or transmitted in any form or by any means, electronic or mechanical, including photocopying and recording, or by any information storage or retrieval system, except as may be expressly permitted in writing by the publisher. Requests for permission should be addressed in writing to LifeWay Press®, One LifeWay Plaza, Nashville, TN 37234.

ISBN 978-1-0877-4239-7
Item 005831548
Dewey Decimal Classification Number: 242
Subject Heading: DEVOTIONAL LITERATURE / BIBLE STUDY AND TEACHING / GOD

Printed in the United States of America

Student Ministry Publishing
LifeWay Resources
One LifeWay Plaza
Nashville, Tennessee 37234

We believe that the Bible has God for its author; salvation for its end; and truth, without any mixture of error, for its matter and that all Scripture is totally true and trustworthy. To review LifeWay's doctrinal guideline, please visit www.lifeway.com/doctrinalguideline.

Unless otherwise noted, all Scripture quotations are taken from the Christian Standard Bible®, Copyright © 2017 by Holman Bible Publishers. Used by permission. Christian Standard Bible® and CSB® are federally registered trademarks of Holman Bible Publishers.

publishing team

Director, Student Ministry
Ben Trueblood

Manager, Student Ministry Publishing
John Paul Basham

Editorial Team Leader
Karen Daniel

Content Editor
Kyle Wiltshire

Production Editor
Brooke Hill

Graphic Designer
Kaitlin Redmond

04 intro

05 getting started

06 what does the bible teach about kindness?

18 how has God shown us kindness?

30 how do we practice kindness?

42 kindness toward the marginalized

76 even if...

table of contents

intro

There is a perception in our world that nice people finish last. Sure, there's the whole virtue signaling thing—publically expressing a politically correct opinion to demonstrate percieved moral character—but when push comes to shove, most people look out for themselves first. In many ways, real, genuine kindness is a lost art.

The Bible is full of direction and instruction on how to express true kindness. We're not just talking about lip service or fake Instagram posts to look like you're a good person. We're talking about real, life-changing kindness. It's not only possible, but it's expected if you are a follower of Christ.

As Jesus' disciples, one of the ways we reveal that we are serious about following Him is how we treat the disenfranchised and marginalized in our world. This book will dive deeply into ways we can do just that; not in a phony way, but in a genuine, Christ honoring way.

This book is divided up into four sections:

I. What does the bible teach about kindness? (Days 1-5)
II. How has God shown us kindness? (Days 6-10)
III. How do we practice kindness? (Days 11-15)
IV. How to show kindness to the marginalized. (Days 16-30)

These next 30 days will challenge you. They will cause you to consider some things that you might have never considered before. And they will help you develop a real kindness that's not based around looking good before others, but in loving God and letting that overflow into love for people.

getting started

This devotional contains 30 days of content, broken down into sections that answer a specific question about Kindness. Each day is broken down into three elements—discover, delight, and display—to help you answer core questions related to Scripture.

discover | This section helps you examine the passage in light of who God is and determine what it says about your identity in view of that. Included here is the key passage, focus Scripture, along with illustrations and commentary to guide you as you study.

delight | In this section, you'll be challenged by questions and activities that help you see how God is alive and active in every detail of His Word and your life. You'll be guided to ask yourself about what the passage means for your relationship with God.

display | Here's where you really take action. Display calls you to apply what you've learned through each day's study.

prayer | Each day also includes a prayer activity in one of the three main sections.

Throughout the devotional, you'll also find extra articles and activities to help you connect with the topic personally, such as Scripture memory verses, additional resources, and questions.

day 1

CHRISTIANS GONNA CHRISTIAN

discover

> As we begin this experience in kindness, let's start with confession before God. Do you desire to be kind? Ask the Holy Spirit to prepare your heart for this. Commit to God your willingness to grow in kindness.

READ COLOSSIANS 3:12-13.

Therefore, as God's chosen ones, holy and dearly loved, put on compassion, kindness, humility, gentleness, and patience. –Colossians 3:12

Here are some facts about kindness: Kindness flows from the Holy Spirit's presence in the Christian's heart, so godly kindness cannot be faked. Saved people practice kindness because they are saved, but they are not saved by acts of kindness. Someone whose heart is far from God could be used by God to show kindness, but these acts of kindness do not save him or her. The kindness of a Christian, however, is kindness for a different reason. We intentionally put on kindness, as Paul said in Colossians, because the Holy Spirit is in us.

Look closely at the first five words of these verses. It all begins with belonging to God. Compassion, kindness, humility, and the other attributes flow from the fact that we belong to God. Notice how logically consistent this is, given the fact that we are, according to verse 12, "holy and dearly loved." We are loving and kind toward others because God is loving and kind toward us.

delight |

Are you certain that you belong to God? If not, confess today that Jesus is Lord (Rom.10:9) and then tell your ministry leader!

What is the connection between the kindness God showed you in your sin and the kindness you are commissioned to show others?

How is an act of kindness that flows from the Holy Spirit in our hearts better than an act of kindness done for the sake of looking good in front of others?

display |

When we grasp the cosmic fact that God loves us dearly, it changes everything. When we see ourselves as God's beloved, we begin to see others through God's eyes, and it elevates the view we have of other people. We begin to see others the way God sees them. God loves the world (John 3:16), and those who belong to Him should love the world, too. Acts of kindness, then, are the natural outflowing of God's love in us.

Plan an anonymous act of kindness; a practical favor, gift, or encouraging word you will give to someone this week. Do it without seeking to receive any credit.

List some of your past acts of kindness which, in all honesty, were about making yourself look good. Then, list past acts of kindness that God brought about through you. What are the differences between these lists?

day 2

LOVING KINDNESS

discover|

READ 1 CORINTHIANS 13:4-7.

Love is patient, love is kind. Love does not envy, is not boastful, is not arrogant.
-1 Corinthians 13:4

You have been uniquely gifted and uniquely called by the Holy Spirit for something important. If you are a Christian, then the Holy Spirit lives within you. If the Holy Spirit lives within you, then you have a unique set of spiritual gifts for ministry. If you use those spiritual gifts, then you have to use them in a loving way.

While we often hear this verse read at weddings, in its original context, it is about how we use spiritual gifts. It appears in the middle of three chapters that are all about spiritual gifts. This is why people often look confused when the reader at the wedding starts talking about "tongues of men and angels" and "resounding gongs." It is vital that we use the gifts the Spirit has given us in a way that is patient and kind; not in a prideful way that is self-seeking. Show kindness because the Spirit of God is in you and expect to receive absolutely nothing in return.

> **Talk to God, asking for His heavenly will to be done, and for Him to reveal to you the good works He has prepared for you this week. Then, ask Him for the strength to follow through with these opportunities to show kindness, knowing that your intention is not to receive recognition or return favors.**

delight

What is love without patience like? What about love that is marked by envy?

What crosses your mind when someone broadcasts his or her acts of kindness on social media? Is it still kindness shown in love?

Describe an act of kindness that is not done in love, but done arrogantly or boastfully.

display

Living out kindness as a fruit of the Spirit is going to take some patience. Prepare your heart for these acts of kindness to be met with indifference or even possibly hostility. Living out kindness is going to take sincere love in your heart for the people you seek to serve. Check your heart for any envy. Read your own past social media posts for boastfulness. Be on your guard for any arrogance that may come from your heart after you have shown kindness.

Do something kind and uplifting today for someone who tests your patience. Remember today's verse!

Repent and apologize if you have broadcast your kindness in the past so as to be arrogant and boastful instead of showing kindness in love like today's text teaches. Then, take a look at what Jesus said in Matthew 6:1-3.

day 3

SHINY SNAKES

discover

READ PROVERBS 26:23-28.

When he speaks graciously, don't believe him, for there are seven detestable things in his heart. –Proverbs 26:25

King Solomon wrote much of the book of Proverbs. Though he was far from perfect himself, the wisdom that came from Solomon was straight from God. In training his sons to be future Kings, he imparted to them training on godly wisdom, which begins with a fear of the Lord (Prov. 1:7). In Proverbs 26, he warned his sons about the hateful person who "disguises himself with his speech and harbors deceit within" (Prov. 26:24).

In the following verses, Solomon would go on to say this hateful person with a "flattering mouth" (Prov. 26:28) would ultimately dig his or her own pit and fall into it (v.27), with his or her evil "revealed in the assembly (v. 26)." Tragically, you will see this often, and sometimes it will happen in the church. The flattering speech of this hateful person is given with "smooth lips" (v.23), showing how incredibly kind he or she would appear. This is fake kindness, which isn't kindness at all. Kindness must be genuine, or it is just the shine of a snake's skin. It may look appealing, but it's dangerous.

delight

In which settings do you tend to fake kindness, when you really wish you could tell the truth?

Whom have you misled in the past with flattering compliments that you did not truly hold in your heart?

What effect does this false kindness have on someone's credibility in the future?

display

Prepare your heart to spot this kind of fake kindness from others in the future, and respond to it with genuine kindness. Protect your heart from being deceived by empty words of flattery from people who appear kind, but are actually just manipulating you. Watch for this same behavior in your own heart. Remember that your actions and words of kindness are strongest when they are not rooted in what you stand to gain from the person to whom you are showing kindness, but in the Holy Spirit's prompting.

Are you showing favoritism to people who could elevate your status, or are you showing kindness to absolutely everyone, regardless of what they could do for you? Evaluate your motives each time you show kindness to someone today. Journal what happens in your heart when you show genuine kindness to someone who has nothing to offer you.

> Ask God to give you discernment into your own heart; to alert you when you are about to give kind words that are really just intended to avoid the awkwardness of the truth, cover your own tracks, or put yourself on good terms with someone who could do something for you.

Be Kind

day 4

LEGENDARY HOSPITALITY

discover

READ ACTS 28:1-6.

The local people showed us extraordinary kindness. They lit a fire and took us all in, since it was raining and cold. –Acts 28:2

The beautiful scene in today's text was made possible by God's ministry through Paul to the Roman centurion (a commanding soldier) onboard his ship that had just wrecked onto the island of Malta. The other soldiers had planned to kill the prisoners, but this centurion had come to like Paul and decided that the prisoners should swim or drift ashore. Paul's gospel testimony saved lives! However, they still had to survive on Malta.

The famous "northeaster" wind (27:14) that still blows today drove the ship to Malta where it was beached. Paul had absolute confidence that everyone would survive because of a vision given to him by God (27:23-26). The local people of Malta lit a fire for them and took them in because it was raining and cold. This kindness was unprompted, and the shipwreck survivors would not likely be able to repay this kindness, having tossed valuables overboard (28:18,19). What a beautiful legacy. The people of Malta are legendary hosts whose hospitality is recorded in the Bible for all-time. This shows that everyone can be kind, Christian or not.

> **Prayerfully reflect on acts of kindness that came to you in your time of greatest need, just like Paul and his shipmates. Then, make a commitment to God that you will be ready to show such kindness to those in need when their ships wash ashore on your beach.**

delight |

In what ways are Paul's vision from God before the shipwreck (Acts 27:23-26) and the kindness shown by the people of Malta connected?

The people of Malta were not Christians (Acts 28:3-5), or not yet Christians (28:7-10). Does God work through only Christians to show kindness to those who need it? Why, or why not?

The word "extraordinary" in this verse is so important. What is the difference between ordinary kindness and extraordinary kindness?

display |

You have seen the legendary kindness of the people at Malta. Now, it is your turn. These incredibly kind people went through great trouble to help shipwrecked strangers, and the Lord blessed them in abundance as a result of the ministry of one lowly prisoner in their midst. God would heal their leader's father through Paul's hands (28:7-10) and then heal everyone else on the island who was sick! However, they could not have known this as they showed extraordinary kindness to the shipwrecked strangers.

Work with your parent(s) or guardian(s) to gather provisions to meet someone's physical needs. Then, pray that there is a minister in the midst through whom God will bring healing and the gospel to those in need. Resolve in light of the extraordinary kindness of the people of Malta to settle not for ordinary kindness, but instead to show extraordinary kindness today.

day 5

WHAT GOES AROUND

discover

> **Start your prayer with praise and thanksgiving; letting gratitude for all of God's daily provisions eclipse all that troubles you. Then, ask God to root out any cruelty in you and for kindness to reign in your heart.**

READ PROVERBS 11:17.

A kind man benefits himself, but a cruel person brings ruin on himself.

The wisdom of Proverbs could have been written yesterday, but these timeless truths are thousands of years old. While following the Proverbs are not guarantees for success, you will find its wisdom to be sound advice. These little poetic couplets are life-hacks from God. You could live ten lifetimes and learn only a fraction of these truths the hard way, or you could read the Proverbs, apply them to your life, and make the most of the only life you have.

Today's Proverb is one of several that contrasts the kind person with the cruel. Look closely at the first half. It is almost counter-intuitive. How does someone who does kind things for others benefit himself? This verse is not to be confused with the idea of "karma." It also should not reconfigure your motivation for kindness. Kindness that is shown for the sole reason of benefiting oneself is manipulation, but kindness shown as an overflow of the Holy Spirit's presence in your life honors God. It also, in the long-run, does bring about benefits. Likewise, those who are cruel to others will ultimately bring ruin that will crash down on him or her.

delight |

What urge naturally comes up in your heart when someone does something kind for you, or says something kind to you?

In what ways have acts of kindness in your past come back to bless you, or your family later?

How have you observed a legacy of cruelty playing out in the end?

display |

Because you live in a world where not everyone submits to the Word of God, you will encounter cruelty. When you do, Proverbs 11:17 may come to your heart. In that moment, and that moment may be right now, avoid the temptation to take delight in the ruin that comes upon the cruel. Rather, take comfort in the first half of the verse as assurance that you are on God's track.

Show kindness to someone today not because you hope to reap this promised benefit, but just because you love Jesus and He told us to love our neighbors. Take a look at Romans 12:18-19 as well. Knowing that the cruel will experience ruin, show grace when cruelty visits you and express gratitude to God when your own kindness benefits you.

Therefore, as God's chosen ones, holy and dearly loved, put on compassion, kindness, humility, gentleness, and patience, bearing with one another and forgiving one another if anyone has a grievance against another. Just as the Lord has forgiven you, so you are also to forgive.

COLOSSIANS 3:12-13

day 6

REFLECTING HIS LIGHT

discover

> God already knows about your sin, but loves you anyway. So, confess freely to Him. Confess, and confess it all. Trust in the atoning work of Christ on the cross, who paid for your sin with His perfect life and rose again in victory over it. Confess sin, abide in God's grace for you, and ask God to ready your heart for this incredible Scripture passage.

READ EPHESIANS 2:1-10.

He also raised us up with him and seated us with him in the heavens in Christ Jesus, so that in the coming ages he might display the immeasurable riches of his grace through his kindness to us in Christ Jesus. –Ephesians 2:6-7

This chapter of Ephesians opens with some striking words. Before Christ, you were actually dead in sin. Such words are offensive in today's culture, which wishes to virtue-signal at every turn. However, this beautiful news is a critical difference between Christianity and every other worldview. While other religious worldviews would seek to equip you with the tools to climb the mountain to heaven, Christianity sees us as dead and incapable of climbing at all. Instead, God reached down and raised us up from our sin. That is the best news you have read all day!

As a recipient of such endless grace, you are to reflect the light of God's loving kindness. We believe the gospel and are saved, but we did none of the work. This text tells us who did all of the lifting. Salvation is an act of kindness from God that flows from the love He had for us even while we were dead in sin. He did this ultimately for His own glory. As the recipients of the immeasurable riches of His grace (v. 7), that kindness reflects off of us and invites others who are still in darkness into the light of His gospel.

delight |

Remembering that these words were written almost 2,000 years ago, how are you connected to the phrase, "in the coming ages…" in verse 7?

Even though we live on Earth, how does being raised up and seated with Jesus impact the way we reflect His light toward others?

display |

If you have been taking credit for your own salvation, attributing it to righteous acts you have performed in the past, prayerfully remove that from your heart now and place it at the foot of the cross. Express gratitude to Christ for raising you up when you were dead in sin.

Intentionally extend this kindness of God to someone else today. It is okay if you are rejected. What matters is that you pass this kindness of the gospel to others. It passed through countless generations to reach you. Now, pass it on to someone else. Don't let this legacy of God's kindness dead-end with you.

JUST MERCY

discover

READ TITUS 3:1-7.

But when the kindness of God our Savior and his love for mankind appeared, he saved us—not by works of righteousness that we had done, but according to his mercy—through the washing of regeneration and renewal by the Holy Spirit.
–Titus 3:4-5

Some books of the Bible were written to vast regions, while others were written to entire churches. Today's text, however, is a Spirit-inspired letter from Paul to just one person. Titus, one of Paul's protégés, was called to appoint elders in towns all over the island of Crete. The people of Crete had a pretty terrible reputation (Titus 1:12). Today, these words hit us squarely in our sense of self-righteousness and have been helpful for people who have shifted from other faiths to belief in the true gospel of Jesus Christ.

Verse 4 changes everything. Since time began, people have been trying to save themselves; but we never have, nor will we be able to. To the Pharisees of Jesus' day, this kind of teaching was so humbling that it was offensive. To the virtue-signaling culture of our day and to the false religions that teach salvation through works, it is just as offensive. To those who have placed their faith in Jesus, it is freedom.

> **Thank God for His loving kindness. Thank Him for saving you not because of your own works of righteousness, but just because of His mercy.**

delight |

Verse 3 describes how evil we were before coming to know Christ. How does that affect your appreciation for verse 4?

What shifts in your heart when you read the words, "he saved us - not by works of righteousness that we had done?"

display |

This chapter of Titus describes our striving, deception, and enslavement to various passions and pleasures. It reads like a blog post describing modern culture today, but it was written nearly 2,000 years ago. The Word of God is always true and relevant. These same words of freedom from legalism—the belief that you can save yourself with righteous acts—are still setting people free today.

When you encounter a worldview such as Islam, Mormonism, or Buddhism, which claim that righteous acts can elevate a person spiritually, have Titus 3:4-5 marked and ready in your Bible to share.

If you use social media, share the beautiful words of freedom found in Titus 3:4-5 with your friends and followers. Let kindness guide your responses if anyone comments on your post.

day 8

GOD'S INEXHAUSTIBLE KINDNESS

discover

READ PHILIPPIANS 4:10-20.

And my God will supply all your needs according to his riches in glory in Christ Jesus. –Philippians 4:19

Today's passage echoes Proverbs 11:7 and sheds light on possibly the most misquoted verse in the Bible, Philippians 4:13. "I am able to do all things through him who strengthens me," is often used to boost one's confidence when facing physical challenges. However, in context, Paul was thanking the church at Philippi for sending him a financial gift that met all of his needs. Paul also shared that he was acquainted with both poverty and plenty.

The people of God at Philippi had given in support of Paul's ministry, but were really giving "a fragrant offering, an acceptable sacrifice, pleasing to God" (Phil. 4:18). In response, Paul gave these comforting and prophetic words that are also true for Christians today. The kindness God supplies for the receiver of the gift will be supplied to the giver as well.

> **Reflect on your life so far. Even if there have been lean times in your family's past, reflect on how God has always provided. Thank God for supplying all of your needs. Rest in the comfort that comes from knowing God's kindness will supply all of your needs.**

Lifeway Students | Devotions

delight

These words were originally written to Christians who had kindly given to Paul's ministry. In what ways can you give to ministry this week?

When people who do not have much give to God, how does God supply all of their needs?

What role does faith play when giving to God?

display

Make it a point to rest in the comfort that comes from knowing your provisions ultimately come from God's "riches in glory in Christ Jesus." Set a timer and dwell for five minutes in thankfulness to your Provider, whose riches never run dry. Spend every minute in a spirit of gratitude, glorifying God, whose loving kindness is inexhaustible.

Stop at your front door to thank God for your home today, even if it seems weird to your family and neighbors. Lay your hands on it and thank God that you have one. Let the gratitude in your heart for God's provision wash away any longing or desire you have toward the things of others.

day 9

REDEMPTION'S COST

discover

> **Thank Jesus for the blood He spilled on the cross to atone for the sins of all who believe in Him. As you would before taking the Lord's Supper at church, tell Him that you remember His broken body and atoning blood. Thank Him for His sacrifice.**

READ EPHESIANS 1:7-10.

In him we have redemption through his blood, the forgiveness of our trespasses, according to the riches of his grace that he richly poured out on us with all wisdom and understanding. - Ephesians 1:7-8

As believers born into the New Testament era, we never had to travel to Jerusalem at Passover and sacrifice a lamb. We never saw its blood spilled symbolically on our behalf. The closest thing we have to this is the cup we drink at the Lord's Supper in remembrance of Jesus' blood. He is the ultimate Lamb; the Lamb of God who takes away the sin of the world (John 1:29). Let us never forget our redemption's cost. It came from the blood of the Perfect One.

Note in verse 8 that this redemption was not poured out frivolously, but "with all wisdom and understanding." Jesus knew precisely what He was doing when He stood silent before His accusers and followed through with the crucifixion. He knew you then. Note the first two words of v.7. This redemption is indeed in Him and Him alone. It is the forgiveness of every last one of your trespasses according to the riches of His kindness.

delight

Why do we need redemption as described in verse 7?

What is the difference betwen worldly wealth and the "riches of his grace" described in verse 7?

What impact does it have on you to realize that your redemption came as a result of the blood of Jesus?

display

Because you have this redemption, it is time to live like one of the redeemed. Because you have been forgiven, it is time to forgive. Because this forgiveness and redemption have been richly poured out on you from the riches of God's grace, it is time to invite others into the kindness of God.

The kindness the Lord poured out on you is where your kindness comes from. With your heart stripped of any shred of pride, look around you right now. Look at every person who you come across the rest of the day through this lens. See the gospel potential and then share the good news. Watch that same grace and kindness that was richly poured out on you be poured out onto others and give God 100% of the glory.

day 10

HELPER OR HYPOCRITE?

discover |

READ ROMANS 2:1-4.

Or do you despise the riches of his kindness, restraint, and patience, not recognizing that God's kindness is intended to lead you to repentance?
–Romans 2:4

Today's culture loves to call out hypocrisy. People on social media can quickly become a mob delighting in exposing another's wrongdoing and piling condemnation onto the humiliated person with self-righteous scorn. Yet, they fail to regard the ironically wrong nature of the hateful frenzy itself. In v.1, Paul warned his Roman readers of this very danger.

To identify your own hypocrisy is a good thing. However, be careful joining in the hoard of angry onlookers when someone else's hypocrisy is exposed. In v.3, Paul reminded the Romans, and us, that neither the sinner nor the hoard calling out his or her sin will escape God's judgment.

God is patient with us and wants us to come to repentance (2 Pet. 3:9). However, we must be careful not to delight in seeing another person fall. Every finger we point at the sinner in the center of a judgmental mob belongs to an equally qualified sinner. And all of us must give an account before the same God whose kindness is designed to bring us all to repentance. God has called us to be helpers, not hypocrites.

Lifeway Students | Devotions

delight

Describe a time when God's kindness in your life led you to repentance.

Is God obligated to show us kindness?

Why is God's judgment based in truth (v.2) while the judgment of a hateful mob is not?

> **Ask God to forgive you for times when you joined in the scornful mob. Ask for God to remind you of these verses the next time you're tempted to join such a mob. Ask for God's grace that overcomes the self-righteous desire to pile on in when someone else is busted for something you have done yourself.**

display

If you live according to this text, it is going to set you apart. In a world that is hungry to humiliate wrongdoers, be one who reaches out a hand to the accused, saying, "I know what it is like to fall." This is radically counter-cultural and very gospel-centered.

Journal a prayer thanking God for His restraint (v. 4) when He saw you sin. Thank God for His patience with you when you fell again and again.

Be Kind

What Kindness Does

When we think about the word kindness in the Bible, typically, this verse comes to mind: "Pleasant words are a honeycomb: sweet to the taste and health to the body" (Prov. 16:24). But kindness is meant for more than our words; kindness is about the way we treat others too.

Kindness Starts Here

Here's the thing: You cannot control what other people do. We live in a fallen world, so sometimes people do incredibly unkind things. With the help of the Holy Spirit, though, we can respond to others with both kindness and self-control (Gal. 5:22-23). Our responses are not mechanical; rather, they are guided by the very Spirit of the God who loves us. He is both our help and our ultimate example of loving kindness (John 14:26; Eph. 2:7). The truth is that we can choose kindness no matter what someone else does or fails to do. When it becomes especially difficult to be kind, first remember that God is and has been kind to us—even when we don't deserve it.

Kindness Is Good for Us

Not only do acts of kindness help others feel valued and seen, but they can also help us by increasing our mood and even our lifespan. Being kind to others even lowers our levels of stress, anxiety, pain, and depression. (https://www.dartmouth.edu/wellness/emotional/rakhealthfacts.pdf) This idea is found in Scripture, too. The Book of Proverbs says, "a kind man benefits himself" (11:17a), and some of those benefits include "life, righteousness, and honor" (21:21).

Kindness Is Good for Others

When we're kind to others, they experience more than a generous action or nice words. Take a look at these ten things the Bible says about what kindness does for others.

- Kindness shows love (1 Cor. 13:4).
- Being kind means extending forgiveness (Eph. 4:32).
- Kindness points others to Jesus (2 Cor. 6:3-13)
- Kindness expects nothing in return (Luke 6:35).

- God's kindness leads to repentance (Rom. 2:4).
- Kindness builds up others (Rom. 15:2).
- Being kind means welcoming and caring for even those we don't know (Acts 28:2).

- When we're kind, we care for the oppressed and marginalized (Isa. 1:17)
- Kindness rejoices with others (Rom. 12:15).
- Kindness restores (2 Sam. 9:7; Rom. 5:8).

Reflect

When have you done something kind for someone else and felt joy because of it?

How might being kind to others take our minds off of our own stress, depression, pain, or anxiety?

What are some ways kindness toward others reflects God's image into the world?

Which of the 10 effects of kindness stood out to you? Why?

If someone looked at your life over the last 24 hours, would they describe you as kind? Why or why not?

If not, how can you begin to choose kindness today?

Section 3: HOW DO WE PRACTICE KINDNESS?

day 11

BEGIN WITH FORGIVENESS

discover

READ EPHESIANS 4:20-32.

And be kind and compassionate to one another, forgiving one another, just as God also forgave you in Christ. –Ephesians 4:32

Forgiveness sets you free. You are free to let go of past pain. You are free to move on from toxic moments in your relationships and to take the risk of trusting people again. Only the gospel makes this truly possible because only the gospel transforms people. It begins with accepting the reality that we are just as stained by sin as those who have sinned against us.

In the verses for today, Paul instructed the Ephesians to take off their old way of living (v.22). Refusing to forgive is from the old way, not the new way of life Jesus calls us to. Grace is the only way a culture of imperfect people can move forward and grow. And there is no greater grace than that of God toward sinners.

If you are going to practice kindness, then you need to be a forgiving person. You are called to give what you have recieved. You have been freely forgiven! So, freely forgive.

delight

In Matthew 5:7, Jesus said, "Blessed are the merciful, for they will be shown mercy." How is this verse similar to Ephesians 4:32?

Lifeway Students | Devotions

Is it possible to be kind, but not compassionate? Why or why not?

display |

You have a simple choice between forgiveness or giving in to bitterness. You will be wronged, and you have wronged others. Remember that God is the author of this exquisite concept. Remember that the forgiveness He offers you begins with the sacrifice of the only One who has never wronged anyone. Look at the chain of forgiveness God has started. Do not leave a legacy of bitterness when your inheritance is forgiveness.

Unless doing so would wound this person, reach out to someone you have wronged. Apologize and seek to make things right. Remember to allow kindness to guide your response to them.

Allow the Holy Spirit to bring your heart to a place of true forgiveness toward those who have hurt you. Unless those who have wronged you have expressed a desire to hear your forgiveness articulated, there is no need to contact them and let them know you forgive them. In fact, this could do damage and, in some cases, could come across as unusual because they often do not realize they have hurt you in the first place.

> **With a physical hand gesture of laying something down, in prayer, lay at God's feet the bitterness you may be holding against someone else. Lay down every wound on your heart that was put there by someone who hurt you. Then, abide in and trust the forgiveness Christ accomplished for you and every last sin for those who believe in Him.**

day 12

FORTITUDE

discover

> Ask God for a refresh from His Spirit. Confess any lingering sin you have been pretending did not happen. Dwell for a moment in the peace that comes from knowing Christ's resurrection guarantees victory and atonement for your every sin. Speak honestly with God about ways in which you are weary, then prepare to be refreshed and encouraged.

READ GALATIANS 6:1-10.

Let us not get tired of doing good, for we will reap at the proper time if we don't give up. Therefore, as we have opportunity, let us work for the good of all, especially for those who belong to the household of faith. –Galatians 6:9-10

What if your football team fought hard to get to the end zone, but just gave up at the one-yard line? What if you pulled an all-nighter on a paper, but just stopped before the conclusion? What if you dropped out of school one week before graduation?

It is especially easy to grow tired of doing good and give up right before the goal if you feel isolated and are not plugged into your church. Your Christian walk is not just about you; it is the part you play in the bigger picture of God's kingdom. Your unique spiritual gifts and contributions are part of a team effort, and that team is the church. So, never give up, never walk alone, and work for the good of your friends at church. You will find that your weariness subsides when you lift up a fellow member of your family of faith.

delight |

List some examples of good works that eventually lead to success in the mission of God, but do not show immediate results.

How can you practice working for the good of those in your household of faith at your local church?

There are huge theological implications to the words "as we have opportunity" (v.10). Who provides these opportunities?

display |

Press on. If you do not give up, you will reap spiritual results! I Corinthians 15:58 says, "Therefore, my dear brothers and sisters, be steadfast, immovable, always excelling in the Lord's work, because you know that your labor in the Lord is not in vain." Your Spirit-filled acts of kindness are never meaningless. Know that you are not the only Christian in the world. God has surrounded you with others, and they need encouragement, too.

Make a list with the names of students and leaders in your church, including your pastor, whom you can encourage today. Even just a few quick words could be used by God to encourage them in a time of need.

day 13

UPSIDE-DOWN WORLD

discover

> **Before you begin today's devotion, ask God to give you an open heart to what He has to say to you through His Word. Regardless of your relationship with your earthly father, You have a Heavenly Father who loves you and is ready to help you do something the world finds unbelievable.**

READ LUKE 6:27-36.

But love your enemies, do what is good, and lend, expecting nothing in return. Then your reward will be great, and you will be children of the Most High. For he is gracious to the ungrateful and evil. –Luke 6:35

Christianity is completely distinctive from other worldviews. In today's Scripture, Jesus said something radical...again. If you aren't yet, get used to God calling you to do the opposite of what secular culture and your flesh tell you to do. He calls us to live in an upside down world.

In v.34, Jesus acknowledged that "Even sinners lend to sinners to be repaid in full." It is perfectly fair to expect to be repaid in full, but it is perfectly Christ-like to give freely and expect nothing in return. He even calls His followers to love their enemies. This is counter-cultural and is exactly what our world needs right now. It's easy to love those who love you. It's difficult to love those who are indifferent toward you, or even those who despise you. It seems drastic, but it is the bare minimum of what Jesus calls us to do.

delight

Have you ever lent something to someone that they didn't return? How did it make you feel?

While Jesus' teaching might be difficult and counter-cultural, He mentions a "reward" (v.35). What reward do you think Jesus is referring to here?

God is described as "the Most High" in v. 35. Because He is the Most High, He calls His people to a different standard. How does knowing that God is the Most High help you live out His standard?

display

We are called to be children who act like our Father. Our Father freely gave, knowing we could never repay our debt. Our Father is gracious to us even when we are ungrateful. He even shows patient grace toward those who are evil, desiring that they come to repentance (2 Peter 3:9). When we do what is good, love our enemies, show kindness as an overflow of the Spirit, and give without expecting a return, we are children who act like our Father.

Keep your eyes open for opportunities to meet needs today. Then, expecting nothing in return, step in, speak up, and serve well.

Journal a statement of your faith in Jesus' promise of a great reward. When the enemy drags you down, revisit this statement because your faith will be tested.

day 14

BOLD HUMILITY

discover

> Tell God how hallowed, or sacred, His name is to you. Pray a prayer that praises Him for how great He is. Watch as both your troubles and your ego shrink in importance and prominence in your heart as you grow in Him.

READ MICAH 6:8.

Mankind, he has told each of you what is good and what it is the Lord requires of you: to act justly, to love faithfulness, and to walk humbly with your God.

The prophet Micah did not mess around. He did not mimimize the message God gave him or apologize for it. In today's verse, he called out all of humanity, and his bold words still ring true today. As God's people, we know better. We know what is expected of us. These ancient words must be brought back into a place of priority in our hearts and lives. He has called us to be boldly humble.

As fickle people whose moods and convictions change because of anything from headlines to low blood sugar levels, we are not the ultimate authority in life. Our opinions do not determine what is true or false. God is the determiner of right and wrong. Only He has the authority and has shared what is good and right through His Word. Indeed, we know what is good and what the Lord requires of us because of His Word. In the New Testament, Jesus gave us only two commands: to love God and to love others (Matthew 22:37-40). This is kindness.

Lifeway Students | Devotions

delight |

In practical terms for you, what does it mean to act justly?

Since we are clearly called to walk humbly with our God, why do so many Christians struggle with humility?

display |

This Old Testament teaching is still true of God's character today. As New Testament believers, our obedience to the commands Jesus gave us—to love God and others (Matt. 22:37-40)—line up exactly with the calling of Micah 6:8: to act justly, love faithfulness, and walk humbly with our God.

It is good to grow and learn when presented with new teachings we have yet to encounter in God's Word, but we cannot love faithfulness and walk humbly with God if we constantly take our marching orders from misguided clutural morality. We must let God's Word guide our interaction and posts on social media. Take a moment to review your recent posts and make sure your heart echoes God's heart, found in Micah 6:8.

When God gives you an opportunity to speak up about the gospel, let these words be branded on your heart. Speak kindly with the humility and boldness Micah displayed.

day 15

RELIGION UNDEFILED

discover

READ JAMES 1:19-27.

Pure and undefiled religion before God the Father is this: to look after orphans and widows in their distress and to keep oneself unstained from the world.
–James 1:27

One of the least-appreciated proofs of Jesus' divinity is the fact that His earthly half brother, one of the biological children of Joseph and Mary and who used to rag on Jesus (John 7:2-9), ultimately called Him "Lord." Just try to get one of your siblings, or friends, to believe that you are God. This brother's name was James, and he wrote the book we will learn from today.

The word "religion" brings up trauma for countless wounded souls. It evokes long legacies of meaningless rituals and rules that bring people no closer to God. However, today's Scripture brings this word back to its purest form. In acts of kindness that grow from us as fruit of the Holy Spirit, we look after orphans and widows in their distress. Because we have been called out by God and set apart, we cannot possibly ever successfully blend in with the spiritual darkness around us. We are to be, "...blameless and pure, children of God who are faultless in a crooked and perverted generation, among whom you shine like stars in the world (Philippians 2:15)..." We are to keep ourselves unstained from the world.

Lifeway Students | Devotions

delight

Because the Word makes clear what pure and undefiled religion is, name some examples you have seen of impure and defiled religion.

How can a Christian actively keep from being stained by the world, but still speak in a way that is clearly understood by the world?

display

It is time to be real with your religion. Not only is it time for the stain-remover of the gospel, but it is time to see impactful results from your faith. Because you are a Spirit-filled Christian, kindness toward orphans and widows will result as fruit of your faith. So, what is it going to be? It is time to live out a new definition, the biblical definition, of the word "religion" to those around you.

Working with your parent or guardian and a pastor or ministry leader, ask about ways you can be a blessing to orphans in your community and widows in your church. Then, actually follow through and practice godly kindness with pure and undefiled religion.

> **Express to God your sincere intent to be uncompromising in your personal holiness as you carry out His mission. Echo to God the words Jesus spoke to His disciples in Matthew 10:16 as you ask for God's help to be as shrewd as a serpent, but as innocent as a dove.**

And be kind and compassionate to one another,

forgiving one another, just as God also forgave you in Christ.

EPHESIANS 4:32

day 16

DON'T INSULT THE MAKER

discover

Pray for those who do not currently have enough to make it through the day. Ask God for opportunities to meet the needs of the most impoverished in your community.

READ PROVERBS 14:31.

The one who oppresses the poor person insults his Maker, but one who is kind to the needy honors him.

People caught up in a culture that does not practice godly kindness will only show respect to those from whom they may get something in return. So, a culture that lacks kindness will utterly neglect the poor because the absolute poorest among us have nothing to give in return. As King Solomon imparted wisdom to his sons to prepare them to hopefully be Kings one day, he pressed upon their hearts the obligation of a king to meet the needs of the poor. He did this by reminding them of Whose the poor are.

Both the oppressor and the poor man have the same Maker, and that Maker is insulted when His creation oppresses a fellow creation. Whether you have much, or little, the things of this world will do us no good when we stand before God. However, it is an act that honors God when you are kind to the poor. Why? It honors God because it imitates God.

delight |

As evidenced by this passage today, God clearly cares for the poor. How can believers live out this proverb today?

How does it honor God when believers show kindness to those in greatest need?

display |

If your motivation in helping those who do not have as much as you is to appear virtuous, then you don't seek to honor God yourself. However, if you seek to apply your life to this verse by honoring God through showing kindness to the poor, then this act of kindness is about something greater than your self-image.

While you may not be actively oppressing the poor, it is easy just to ignore them and assume they're not your problem. If you have the opportunity to help someone but refuse, you've participated in ignoring their needs, and this is an insult to God.

Pack a sack lunch or two and put them in you or your parent's car. Include items you can find around your house that won't quickly spoil like a bottle of water, granola or protien bar, or a bag of chips. Consider writing out an encouraging Bible verse, like Romans 15:13, on an index card and adding it to the bag. When you see someone in need, give them one of your sack lunches and encourage them.

day 17

BLESSING JESUS

discover

> **Open with a prayer of gratitude for all that you have, even if it is not much compared to others.**

MATTHEW 25:37-40.

And the King will answer them, 'Truly I tell you, whatever you did for one of the least of these brothers and sisters of mine, you did for me.'-Matthew 25:40

Christians have a greater obligation to care for the marginalized than the secular world possibly could. In fact, when non-Christians practice such kindness, they are actually borrowing from Christianity. All people are made in the image of God, but all people are also stained with sin. When one who does not know Chirst does something from "the goodness of their heart" they are operating out of thier original programming—God's image—over their sin nature.

As a follower of Christ, the new life you have in Jesus calls you to live opposite of your sin nature at all times. Your reason for voluntarily feeding the hungry, giving a drink to the thirsty, helping people find housing, providing clothing to those who need it, and caring for the sick is because Jesus is your Lord. When you do these things, you bless Jesus. This is a higher calling than any self righteous behavior done to impress others or give off the impression that you are a virtuous person.

delight

Why is it important to show such kindness "to the least of these" and not only to those who could pay you back or elevate your status?

Why do you think Jesus refers to the poor, sick, and imprisoned as His brothers and sisters?

Why does Jesus' instruction to care for those in need apply to both those who have much and those who do not?

display

There will always be those who have more than you, so do not take the devil's bait and get sucked into the meaningless rat race to accumulate more and more stuff. If you take a global perspective, if you have a roof over your head and a phone, you are more wealthy than most of the people who have ever lived. That puts things in a different perspective when you think it about it.

In light of this text, what opportunity is God presenting to you when you serve someone who has less than you? Is it an opportunity to look good before others, or is it an opportunity to bless Jesus Himself? When you do get the opportunity to serve someone this week, don't rush to social media to tell everyone about it. Your Father in heaven knows. That is enough.

Those who wait until they are rich to give to the poor sometimes struggle to follow through when they finally have wealth. God calls us to be generous. Begin practicing generosity now, even as a teenager.

day 18

THE RIGHTEOUS POOR

discover

READ PROVERBS 28:6.

Better the poor person who lives with integrity than the rich one who distorts right and wrong.

If given the choice between being rich or poor, most people would choose to be rich. There certainly can be comforts and opportunities that come along with wealth. Unfortunately, wealth can also distort one's perspective on morality. Being rich can cause people to feel they are "above the law" or able to buy their way out of trouble. For this reason, the verse for today explains that it's better to be poor and have integrity, than to be wealthy and have a corrupted view of right and wrong.

Clearly, not all rich people distort right and wrong, and some poor people have backwards morality as well. The point of the verse is that godly integrity is of utmost importance. It's not saying that poverty is better than wealth. Wealth, like anything, must be submitted to the Lordship of Christ. Anything that we allow to take center stage in our lives can cause us to distort right and wrong.

Ultimately, wealth is infinitely less important than your integrity. When you stand before God one day, He will be totally unimpressed with the physical items you collected during your lifetime. He created the world, remember? He owns it all already.

delight

How does wealth, or anything we place before God, cause us to distort what is right and wrong?

In what way, specifically, is the poor person with integrity better off than the morally bankrupt wealthy person?

display

We live in a temporary world facing a coming eternal Kingdom. When we compromise our consciences and ignore the Holy Spirit's conviction, we may succeed temporarily, but we are choosing to succeed where it does not matter. Doing sinful things that help us in worldly terms causes us to fail where it matters forever. The good news is that there is grace found in Jesus. But first, we must repent of our wrong doing.

If you are struggling with envy toward those who have more than you, let it go. Give it to God right now. If you have watched people who distort right and wrong succeed in this life, let God deal with them and focus your heart on Him. Strive to make your heart's cry, "The riches of the corrupt wealthy are out of my control. I will stop worrying about them and focus on my own heart."

Today's verse says that it is better to have your integrity even if you have little. Journal two visions of your future self as an adult; one in which you are wealthy and one in which you are not. May both of your journal entries describe a godly person of integrity who shows kindness to those who have less.

> **Make the commitment to God in prayer that, regardless of how much or how little you have as an adult one day, you will always have integrity.**

day 19

LITTLE + RIGHTEOUSNESS = BETTER

discover

READ PSALM 37:1-29.

The little that the righteous person has is better than the abundance of many wicked people. –Psalm 37:16

Today's verse from the Psalms, sounds like a Proverb. King David, the author of Psalm 37, was a master at blending the wisdom of God with the beauty of poetry. This psalm speaks to the futility of wickedness. Four times David explained who would "inherit the land" (vv. 9,11,22,29). In each instance, those who would inherit the land were ones who put their hope in the Lord, the humble, those blessed by the Lord, and the righteous. In each situation, David highlighted one's posture before God as most important.

Our previous devotion focused on integrity being greater than material wealth. This verse focuses on the material wealth of the righteous, contrasting it with the material wealth of the wicked. What we do with what we have indicates what is happening in our hearts; for better or for worse. The righteous person will use even what little he or she has to honor God by showing kindness to others, while the wicked will use their abundant wealth for fruitless or evil endeavors. Once again, God's Word plainly reveals that it's better to have little and be righteous before God than to have much and be wicked.

delight

If someone lives righteously before God, what will ultimately come from their material wealth on earth, regardless of it is much or little?

What good will riches be to the wicked when they come to the end of their lives and see God face to face?

display |

The righteous person in Psalm 37:16 may not have much, but he or she will show kindness to those in need because of the Holy Spirit who lives inside of them. After all, only the Holy Spirit can transform a wicked person into a righteous person. Every righteous person was once wicked.

Write down the last three items you purchased. What was the purpose of those items? Were they truly necessary?

Utimately, we must see everything we have as belonging to God. Whether it is much or little, it's His. We must also believe that God is the great multiplier. He can take even a little bit and do great things with it (see Matt. 14:18-21). Write down three ways you can use whatever resources you have (great or small) to show kindness to others.

> **Talk honestly to God about what you have and what you will have one day. Ask God to help you see that whatever you have or will have, will always belong to God. Make it your heart's desire to use whatever you have for righteousness rather than wickedness.**

day 20

JUSTICE AND THE JUDGE

discover

READ PSALM 140:12-13.

I know that the Lord upholds the just cause of the poor, justice for the needy.
–Psalm 140:12

Statements about injustice presuppose that rights were violated or that promises were broken. So, any meaningful statement about justice presupposes that someone gave us rights and made us promises. The ideals that guide nations with justice systems must draw their authority from an ultimate understanding of justice in the universe. Where there is justice, there is the Judge. Ultimately, justice derives from the existence of a real God who cares about people and created our understanding of right and wrong.

Unfortunately, modern society has fired God as the Judge, but still longs for justice. Inately, we all have the same general sense of what is right and what is wrong. We, as a culture, should not have turned our back on Him like countless other failed societies have in the past across the millennia.

However, the gospel always gives us hope. God has brought revival to failing nations in the past, and Christians today can reintroduce the forgotten gospel that gives true hope to the poor; hope not in a government system that cannot change hearts, but in a Savior whose Spirit permanently transforms souls.

delight

How does God uphold the cause of the poor and give justice to the needy in our day?

What role should the church play in upholding the cause of the poor and seeking justice for the needy?

display

Those in power will answer to God for what they did for the poor and needy in their care. You may not be in a position of power, but God's Spirit is in you and you can speak these words of hope to those who are victims of injustice, circumstance, or even victims of their own sin. God cares about the poor. He hears their cries and upholds their cause. Join Him in that mission.

When your friends or classmates talk about justice, direct the conversation to the ultimate origins of justice itself. Get down to the very roots of where justice comes from in the first place. God created justice and put it in our hearts to long for it.

Hide this verse in your heart. Use pages 64-65 to help you memorize it. When you see headlines about needy people being oppressed, let it remind you of God's position on the matter. Let it lead you to take the same positon. Use your life to uphold the cause of the poor and seek justice for the needy.

> **Ask God to give you hope for ultimate justice to be done one day for those in need. Profess to Him your belief that these words are absolutely true and let them give you peace; peace that you can share.**

Simple Acts of Kindness

Kindness isn't just a topic of discussion in the Bible, and it's more than a character trait or superlative. Kindness is a choice to take action. Maybe you've heard stories of people buying someone else's coffee, gas, or food and put those ideas on a pedestal of the best ways to show kindness. While those are great things to do for others if you can, there are simple, everyday ways we can show kindness, too.

Here are Fifteen Ways to Choose Kindness Today

1 Carry groceries inside for an elderly neighbor.

2 Offer to babysit for a single mom or young couple—for free!

3 Write a thank-you note to someone who showed you kindness.

4 Invite the new kid to sit with you at lunch or at church.

5 Pay a compliment to someone you don't know.

6 Try not to complain about anything for the whole day.

7 Give your time to someone who's lonely.

8 Go through your clothes and donate anything you've outgrown or don't wear often.

9 If someone else begins to gossip, don't participate. Instead, encourage them to go directly to that person or not to talk about them.

10 Set aside your phone when spending time with your family and friends.

11 Do a shout out post for one person each day this month on social media, sharing about what makes them awesome!

12 Think about your favorite songs, podcasts, movies, books, and videos. Consider which of your friends might enjoy them and send them a link or let them borrow the book or movie.

13 Ask your pastor for the name of a senior adult who might be a shut-in or doesn't have family in the area. Begin building a relationship with this person; it'll be good for you, too!

14 Buy an extra coffee or hot chocolate and give it to someone you know is having a tough day. Consider finding out their favorite flavor and buying that. Attach a short note or encouraging Bible verse.

15 Say thank you to people who don't hear it often—like the people who clean the restrooms at your school or serve the food. Consider writing them a note too.

Now it's your turn. Ask God to show you how you can use the gifts He's given you to show kindness to others. Think about your life, the people around you, and the opportunities you have to choose kindness. Make a list of at least five more simple ways you can show kindness.

day 21

BLESSED IMMIGRANT

discover

READ LEVITICUS 23:22.

"When you reap the harvest of your land, you are not to reap all the way to the edge of your field or gather the gleanings of your harvest. Leave them for the poor and the resident alien; I am the Lord your God."

Israel is a unique nation, and its roots in the Old Testament established them originally as a nation led by God himself; a theocracy. Their very laws were written by God, and one of those laws called them to care for the poor and the immigrants by allowing them to gather what was leftover after each harvest.

An act of kindness toward the poor, established in Leviticus, played a key role in the coming of the Messiah. In the Book of Ruth, an immigrant widow from an enemy nation followed her mother-in-law to her home in Bethlehem. She arrived just in time for the barley harvest. Because the farmers observed this law from Leviticus 23:22, she and her mother-in-law had more than enough to eat.

However, this was about far more than a meal. The owner of the field was a man named Boaz. This young widow was named Ruth. These were the great-grandparents of King David. Their greatest descendant, however, is Jesus. Ruth and Boaz would not have met were it not for today's verse and Boaz's commitment to show kindness to the needy.

Lifeway Students | Devotions

delight |

Why did God remind His Old Testament people that He is the Lord at the end of this command?

What does this command reveal about the heart of God toward the poor and the alien in ancient Israel's day?

What does this command reveal about the heart of God toward the poor and the alien today?

display |

Even if a nation had zero laws requiring people to care for the poor and the immigrants, it would still fall to Christians to care for them voluntarily. Moreover, modern laws that force people to give to the poor and to the immigrant do nothing to address the heart of the giver. Only the gospel can transform a heart and fill a former sinner with the Holy Spirit, which leads to acts of kindness toward the marginalized. No modern law that provides assistance for an immigrant can address the spiritual needs of the downtrodden: only Jesus can do that. So, Christians of all nations have to step up.

Speak to your parent, guardian, and/or ministry leader about ways your church can help to care for immigrants. Then, volunteer on the spot to help!

day 22

CREATOR IN COMMON

discover

> Ask the Holy Spirit to reveal to you any prejudice that is in your heart toward those on the other end of the wealth spectrum from you and your family, whether rich or poor. Listen closely to how He convicts you and prepare your heart to read God's Word on the matter.

READ PROVERBS 22:1-2.

Rich and poor have this in common: the Lord makes them all. –Proverbs 22:2

Our spiritual need for a Savior is an incredible equalizer. All the wealth in the world could not save a sinner, and even the most virtuous poor person in the world still needs Christ. Whether we spend our lives accumulating impressive things or giving away all we have, we are all still born equally sinful and in need of a Savior.

Note the stark contrast at the beginning of this verse and the unifying truth at the end. Our culture needs to be reminded of this teaching. Those who look down on the poor need to know that their wealth does not give them greater standing in the eyes of God. Those who have struggled materially in this world should recognize the wealthy as their fellow creations. While many want to label people as many ways as possible, today's Scripture reminds us of two simple truths—God made everyone and the ground is level at the foot of the cross. These are beautiful truths.

delight

Why does our culture assign different values to people based on how wealthy they are?

What does a right understanding of this verse do to the practice of valuing people based on their incomes?

What else do the rich and poor have in common?

display

Let this verse be a set of glasses through which you view wealth inequality. All wealth and all poverty are temporary. Salvation is eternal. People have value because they are made in the image of God and loved by Him—not because of the amount of stuff they have. View the wealthy not with contempt or undue admiration. View the poor not with disdain or inappropriate sainthood. View all as creations of our loving God in need of salvation.

Because both the wealthy and the poor came from the same Creator, they will also answer to the same Judge; hopefully as Savior. Write down three steps you can take to place money in the place it needs to be in your heart.

Keep mental track of the ways you speak to people based on their wealth. If you find yourself speaking more kindly to wealthy people and less charitably toward poor people, confess that before God and repent in light of this verse.

Be Kind

day 23

FAVORITISM

discover

Ask for God's forgiveness for any instance of showing favoritism you have ever committed. Allow today's scripture to guide your thoughts toward God's feelings about favoritism.

READ JAMES 2:1-13.

Listen, my dear brothers and sisters: Didn't God choose the poor in this world to be rich in faith and heirs of the kingdom that he has promised to those who love him? –James 2:5

God's Word calls us out if we treat poor people differently from the way we treat rich people. It's called "showing favoritism" in the book of James. James 2:5 is directed at people whose economic system worked differently from our world's. Today, it is possible to earn money and oppress zero people in the process. The wealthy original recipients of James obtained their wealth through oppressive means and were called out for it.

Under the inspiration of the Holy Spirit, James went on to write, "... you show favoritism, you commit sin and are convicted by the law as transgressors" (v.9). This teaching reminds the rich of the infinite value the poor have in God's eyes. The poor have a dependency on God that is difficult for the rich to grasp. It also challenges the rich to see the poor through God's eyes. Anyone who loves God is an heir to the kingdom and worthy of love, regardless of his or her economic status.

Lifeway Students | Devotions

delight

How is it possible for people to be poor financially but rich in faith?

Heirs are people who inherit wealth from their parents. What does it mean that the poor can be heirs to the kingdom?

A promise is only as good as the integrity of the promise-maker. Why can we trust the promise found in James 2:5?

display

Any Christian of any income level is an heir to the kingdom of God. This makes the poorest Christian in the world infinitely richer in eternity than the richest celebrity heiress with the richest dad in the world.

Think about ways you might inadvertently show favoritism in your school, student ministry, family, and social circles. Write three ways to cease this behavior, even if it's accidental.

If you have been guilty of looking down on those who happen to have come from families with fewer material blessings than yours, let today's text correct the matter in your heart. Ask God to help you see the poor who love God as heirs to a kingdom greater than the greatest wealth in the world, and commit to treat them accordingly.

day 24

NEW MATH

discover

READ LUKE 6:20-26.

Then looking up at his disciples, he said: Blessed are you who are poor, because the kingdom of God is yours. Blessed are you who are hungry now, because you will be filled. Blessed are you who weep now, because you will laugh. –Luke 6:20-21

You may have sat down with your parents to get some help on your math homework, and as you explain what you're learning, been surprised by their response. "This is not how I was taught math!" has been the cry from many kitchen tables, as parental confusion and frustration spilled over while they try to learn how you do math. In many ways, this is how people felt when Jesus came on the scene. His teaching was different from what was accepted as normal. This is the setting for the Scripture for today.

As He did in Matthew 5-7, Jesus turned the common cultural thinking completely upside down in Luke 6 and showed all of us just how drastically we fall short of the biblical Law. This reveals our profound need for a Savior. His words, though, gave hope to a stricken people by turning their weary eyes heavenward to the kingdom awaiting those who place their faith in Him. That same hope remains today. There is no affliction brought on by hunger, poverty, or sadness that is not completely eclipsed by the utter glory of heaven (2 Cor. 4:17).

delight

How does knowing that there is no hunger in heaven bring comfort today?

What are some other examples of Jesus' teaching that are opposite to what is accepted as normal to society? (Hint: Keep reading Luke 6)

display

In Luke 6:20, Jesus told the believing poor that the kingdom of heaven was theirs. As you take action to show kindness to the marginalized, do not meet only their temporary needs to the neglect of eternal needs.

With your parent or guardian's permission and supervision, purchase a $10 gift card from a fast food restaurant and give it to someone asking for help on the street. Explain that you are giving them this gift because you love them and because Jesus loves them, too. See if a spiritual conversation might ensue. Listen to their story and don't judge why they are in the situation they are in. See if you can continue a relationship with them and seek to meet both their physical and spiritual needs.

If you are hungry, weeping, or poor right now, press the very words of Jesus to your heart. Let Him speak directly to your broken heart through this text. Read Revelation 21:1-7 to get a glimpse of what awaits you in heaven, and let the brilliant light bursting from that glimpse obliterate the darkness you may feel. God will provide for your needs. He always has. He always will.

> **Ask God for opportunities to show kindness to those in need—kindness that includes the gospel. Profess your belief to Him that what He said is true.**

day 25

LOCKING EYES

discover

Thank God for providing you and your family what you need to get through the day. Then, ask Him to prepare your heart to help feed the homeless in your city.

READ PROVERBS 28:27.

The one who gives to the poor will not be in need, but one who turns his eyes away will receive many curses.

It is so easy to turn and look away from problems we could solve and people we could help. Sometimes, helping is hard. However, remember that God did not turn and look the other way from us, but gave His only Son as a sacrifice for our sins. This reality obligates us to show kindness and love.

This is an Old Testament text, meaning it was taught under the Old Covenant before Jesus. But what it teaches us about the heart, character, and nature of God still applies. The ancient wisdom of Proverbs will never expire. The first half of the verse reveals something powerful about God's provision for those who are kind and generous to the poor. The curses in the second half of the verse are described as "many" because someone who turned his eyes away from the poor and refused to help was in outright disobedience to the Old Testament Law. While we are no longer under the Old Testament Law, God's righteous anger with those who see the poor and then look away, remains.

delight

Why will the one who gives to the poor not be in need?

What does the turning away of one's eyes indicate?

This verse reveals the necessity of generosity and selflessness for followers of Christ. How can you cultivate generosity and selflessness in your life?

display

Choose not to look away, even though looking away would be easier. Thank God for the ways in which you are not in need. Thank Him for the blessings He gave you after you blessed others—blessings you did not realize He bestowed on you until today's text revealed it to you.

Working with your parent or guardian and ministry leader, volunteer to feed the homeless through a licensed and established facility. When you do, make it a point to look people in the eye and seize any opportunity that may come to hear their stories. Brace yourself: their stories will not likely be G-rated. Like yesterday's Display activity, don't be the judge of why someone is in the place they are in. Just love them and seek to make a friend.

I know that the
Lord upholds
the just cause of
the poor,

justice for the needy.

PSALM 140:12

day 26

GENEROSITY > STINGINESS

discover

READ DEUTERONOMY 15:1-11.

Give to him, and don't have a stingy heart when you give, and because of this the Lord your God will bless you in all your work and in everything you do. For there will never cease to be poor people in the land; that is why I am commanding you, 'Open your hand willingly to your poor and needy brother in your land.' –Deuteronomy 15:10-11

Have you ever read two verses from the Bible that seem to directly contradict one another? Deuteronomy 15:4-5 gave Israel instructions for how they could eliminate poverty completely. These instructions were dependent upon their complete and careful obedience to everything God commanded. If they obeyed God's command, the goal of verse 4, "There will be no poor among you," could be accomplished. Seven verses later came our verses for today. So, what gives?

Because God knew they were incapable of obeying everything He commanded, they would always have poor people among them. Regardless, the economic instructions in Deuteronomy 15 were a path toward the alleviation of all poverty. Notice how this path is not a cold set of bland instructions. No, God's instructions were to care for the poor and to give from their hearts—hearts that were not stingy. This is critical.

delight

Why does the heart of the giver matter to God? Why is it not enough to just give?

God's instructions for Israel's hearts became their nation's laws. How should people who live in nations without such laws take care of their poor?

> **Ask God for an opportunity to earn some money that you will then give to the poor.**

display

When you receive a paycheck, if you have not already, you may see a portion taken out before it comes to you. Some of that deduction goes toward taxes that give assistance to help the poor. But we cannot sit back and think we've done our job because of this. Christians are called to give to our churches, and our churches are called to use some of these resources to serve the poor in your community. Ask your church staff about ways your church helps the poor in your community. Some churches collect a specific fund for this referred to as "benevolence," but your church may go about it differently.

If you do not have a job, create one with the purpose of giving to your church's benevolence ministry or a ministry that serves the poor. Mow someone's lawn, help someone move, wash someone's dog, or take advantage of whatever opportunity you see to earn money. Then, with a generous heart, give to your church's ministry that helps the poor and watch what God does.

day 27

START OFF ON THE RIGHT FOOT

discover

READ PROVERBS 31:8-9.

Speak up for those who have no voice, for the justice of all who are dispossessed.
–Proverbs 31:8

In marching band, there is a concept that is vital to everything else. You might be able to play an instrument to perfection, but if you can't march in step, you will struggle to make it. Whether you've ever marched in a band or not, you can grasp this concept. Watch a parade next Thanksgiving Day on TV or pay attention to the band at halftime of the next football game you attend and marvel as the members of the band seamlessly move with precision; right, left, right, left, right, left.

The key to marching in step is to start off on the right foot. The Scripture we read today is geared to help a young king start off on the right foot.

Except for young royals who inherited their thrones at an early age, everyone who has ever been in power has had to wait for it. You are not yet in power, but that does not mean that you are powerless. You need to start off on the right foot now. If you do not speak up at this stage in your life for those who have no voice—people like the unborn, the poor, and the truly disenfranchised—you will not suddenly start speaking for them when you are an adult and potentially in a position of influence.

delight

Prov. 31:9 calls for us to "defend the cause of the oppressed and needy." Who are the oppressed and needy in our culture?

Using whatever influence you might have, what steps can you take today to speak up for those who have no voice?

display

Find your voice and let it ring out freedom in Christ. Speak with righteous boldness because of the redemption you have in Christ. Roar like a lion (Prov. 28:1). Do not waste words with meaningless phrases (Ecc. 6:11). Do not misrepresent or belittle others. Do not speak anonymously. Do not be afraid of the arrows that come your way for speaking up. Be warned: some arrows may come from other Christians who are afraid to speak the way you do.

If you have followed-through on the challenges presented to you so far in this devotional, you have worked hard to earn money to give to those in need. So, with integrity, you can do it again and enlist others to help you on an even larger scale. Use whatever platform you have, no matter how small, to invite others into this ministry. Just make sure you are not doing anything for your own glory, but only for God's.

> **Pray that you would have a broken heart for the things that break God's heart. Pray that you would have the boldness to speak up for justice when the time comes. Pray that you will speak in love.**

day 28

PRAYERS OF THE DESTITUTE

discover

READ PSALM 102:12-17.

He will pay attention to the prayer of the destitute and will not despise their prayer. –Psalm 102:17

Have you ever taken a device apart because it was broken, fixed it, and then put it back together again? It is amazing to see the inner-workings of something that was designed for a specific purpose. You can clean out the dust and lint that does not belong. You can meticulously repair it and watch it come back to its original purpose. This is what God was doing with Israel when today's text was written.

The psalmist who wrote this was in despair and crying out to God while simultaneously continuing to believe and trust in these beautiful truths about God. The verse immediately before this verse gives important context: "for the Lord will rebuild Zion; he will appear in his glory (v.16)." The name "Zion" refers to Israel and, just like the text prophesied, God did indeed rebuild her.

> **If you have felt or currently feel "destitute," let the truth of this verse wash over you. Believe it. God knows absolutely all about your troubles and this verse states overtly that He is listening. He loves you. So, talk to Him.**

delight |

What types of prayers does God despise? Why would God despise these prayers?

In Psalm 102:1-2, the psalmist speaks very plainly and directly to God. What is the difference between speaking honestly with God and speaking disrespectfully to Him?

display |

A hard lesson to learn is that God sometimes allows us to walk through difficult days. Down the road, the things we learned during those hard days will help us (or someone else) through a time of struggle. Whether we are living in good days or "destitute" days, we must believe that God is still good. He is with us even when we find ourselves crying out in anguish like the psalmist.

Showing kindness to the destitute around you might include sharing this passage of scripture with them, praying with them, or simply sitting and listening to them. Look for someone around you that is struggling. Pause and ask God how you can be an encouragement to them. Then, obey and reach out. God desires for us to bear one another's burdens.

day 29

AWKWARD... BUT NECESSARY

discover

Thank Jesus for giving Himself up for you. Commit to giving what you can to Him.

READ 2 CORINTHIANS 8:7-15.

For you know the grace of our Lord Jesus Christ: Though he was rich, for your sake he became poor, so that by his poverty you might become rich.
-2 Corinthians 8:9

Many critics of Christianity often say that all pastors ever talk about at church is money. While it's not all that is ever discussed at church it is an important element. Pastors, who lead congregations, know the needs of the church, community, and even the world. These needs are met by the tithes and offerings of the people of the church. Without giving, these needs don't get met.

In the Scripture for today, Paul reminded the church at Corinth how Jesus came from heaven to earth in an epic downgrade from incalculable wealth to incredible humility in a manger. Earlier, the Corinthian church had pledged to give an offering for the needs of the Macedonian church. So, Paul appealed heavily to them in these chapters of 2 Corinthians to complete the gift and to give generously the way Jesus gave generously. When we grasp what Jesus did for us—sacrificing Himself completely—we are more apt to surrender everything to Him, including our finances.

delight

Is this verse a promise that God will give you lots of money? What did Paul mean by "rich?"

Why did Paul describe Jesus' descent from the wealth of heaven to the poverty of earth as "grace?"

Describe what happens in your heart when you read the words "for your sake."

display

In 2 Corinthians 9:12, Paul continued, "For the ministry of this service [their financial gift] is not only supplying the needs of the saints but is also overflowing in many expressions of thanks to God." Giving is a form of both kindness and worship. Pray for your pastor the next time he has to encourage the church to give. Sympathize with the awkward yet God-driven position he is in as he pursues the same exact mission that Paul was undertaking as he wrote to the Corinthians 2,000 years ago. If you can find him after worship, give him a word of encouragement.

Each time you earn money, start giving at least 10% of it to your church's general budget. Do it with the same cheerful heart Paul describes in these chapters of 2 Corinthians. Think about the ways God will use it to advance His kingdom and know there is no better use of our money. It is all God's anyway—just like our hearts.

day 30

CALLING HIS SHOT

discover

READ LUKE 4:16-21.

The scroll of the prophet Isaiah was given to him, and unrolling the scroll, he found the place where it was written: The Spirit of the Lord is on me, because he has anointed me to preach good news to the poor. He has sent me to proclaim release to the captives and recovery of sight to the blind, to set free the oppressed, to proclaim the year of the Lord's favor. –Luke 4:17-19

Have you ever seen old social media posts by celebrities from before they were famous, in which they claimed that they would one day become exactly what they are today? It is incredibly inspiring. It is also simultaneously satisfying and sad to read the hateful comments on those posts from the now embarrassed people who told them that they were delusional. On an eternally greater scale, the same thing happened with Jesus.

After Jesus said this to the people at the synagogue in his old hometown of Nazareth, He sat down (which was the traditional posture of teaching) and said, "Today as you listen, this Scripture has been fulfilled" (v. 21). While they were impressed with His gracious words (v. 22), they did not believe Him, and eventually tried to push Him off a cliff for what He said in verse 30. Jesus did every single thing this ancient prophecy said the Messiah would do, including preaching good news to the poor.

For a man coming to change the world, beginning His public life with a declaration of ministry to the poor doesn't seem like the greatest strategy. But if we've learned anything about Jesus, He was anything but ordinary in everything He did.

delight |

What type of captivity do you think Jesus came to release people from?

Why do you think Jesus focused His ministry on the poor and the outcast?

> **Just take a moment and focus your heart on Jesus, your Savior. Praise Him for His kindness to you and ask Him to help you be kind to others in return.**

display |

As you continue to study the fruit of the Holy Spirit, continue to show kindness. We do not get to choose which aspects of the Spirit we bear fruit in and which ones we neglect. So, challenge yourself now with a list of new routines you can build into your year that carry on and even build upon the acts of kindness you have shown so far.

List 5 things you can do to continue to live in kindness.

Even If...

We were created with the ability to reason and choose. Think about the way sin entered the world, it was through the choice Adam and Eve made to disobey God (Gen. 3:6). Yes, Satan tempted them, but ultimately, they knew what God had said and they chose to ignore it in favor of what they wanted in that moment (Gen. 2:17). When we're faced with the temptation to respond in kindness or some other (likely sinful) way, we can choose to be kind.

One critical note here before we dig into some responses Scripture demonstrates for us: You can be hurt and be kind, and you can also disagree and be kind.

Now, let's take a look at some different scenarios Scripture gives for choosing kindness.

I can choose kindness when someone mistreats me.
"Bless those who curse you, pray for those who mistreat you."
—Luke 6:28

I can choose kindness when I face persecution for my faith.
Bless those who persecute you; bless and do not curse.
—Romans 12:14

I can choose kindness when someone gossips about me.
Keep your tongue from evil and your lips from deceitful speech.
—Psalm 34:13

Remind them to submit to rulers and authorities, to obey, to be ready for every good work, to slander no one, to avoid fighting, and to be kind, always showing gentleness to all people.
—Titus 3:1-2

I can choose kindness by not gossiping about someone else.
Without wood, fire goes out; without a gossip, conflict dies down.
—Proverbs 26:20

I can choose kindness by speaking the truth about others to defeat rumors and lies.
"You must not spread a false report. Do not join the wicked to be a malicious witness."
— Exodus 23:1

I can choose kindness by standing up for those who are bullied, mistreated, left out, or overlooked.
Speak up for those who have no voice, for the justice of all who are dispossessed. Speak up, judge righteously, and defend the cause of the oppressed and needy.
—Proverbs 31:8-9

Learn to do what is good. Pursue justice. Correct the oppressor. Defend the rights of the fatherless. Plead the widow's cause.
—Isaiah 1:17

I can choose kindness by avoiding crude jokes.
Obscene and foolish talking or crude joking are not suitable, but rather giving thanks.
—Ephesians 5:4

Avoid irreverent and empty speech, since those who engage in it will produce even more godlessness, and their teaching will spread like gangrene.
—2 Timothy 2:16-17a

I can choose kindness by not arguing with others over things that don't matter.
But reject foolish and ignorant disputes, because you know that they breed quarrels. The Lord's servant must not quarrel, but must be gentle to everyone, able to teach, and patient, instructing his opponents with gentleness.
—2 Timothy 2:23-25

I can choose kindness by speaking compassionately to others.
Pleasant words are a honeycomb: sweet to the taste and health to the body.
—Proverbs 16:24

I can choose kindness by being a good friend.
A friend loves at all times, and a brother is born for a difficult time.
—Proverbs 17:17

I can choose kindness by speaking the truth in love.
But speaking the truth in love, let us grow in every way into him who is the head—Christ.
—Ephesians 4:15

I can choose kindness by choosing to love others like Jesus would.
Love is patient, love is kind.
—1 Corinthians 13:4a

I can choose kindness by forgiving others—no matter what they've done.
And be kind and compassionate to one another, forgiving one another, just as God also forgave you in Christ.
—Ephesians 4:32

Therefore, as God's chosen ones, holy and dearly loved, put on compassion, kindness, humility, gentleness, and patience, bearing with one another and forgiving one another if anyone has a grievance against another. Just as the Lord has forgiven you, so you are also to forgive.
—Colossians 3:12-13

Your Turn

What are some other scenarios where you might need to choose kindness? Support your answer(s) with Scripture.

Notes